THE SUMMER WINDS

Frank Pugliese

BROADWAY PLAY PUBLISHING INC
New York
www.broadwayplaypub.com
info@broadwayplaypub.com

THE SUMMER WINDS
© Copyright 2001 Frank Pugliese

All rights reserved. This work is fully protected under the copyright laws of the United States of America. No part of this publication may be photocopied, reproduced, stored in a retrieval system, or transmitted, in any form or by any means, electronic, mechanical, recording, or otherwise, without the prior permission of the publisher. Additional copies of this play are available from the publisher.

Written permission is required for live performance of any sort. This includes readings, cuttings, scenes, and excerpts. For amateur and stock performances, please contact Broadway Play Publishing Inc. For all other rights please contact the author c/o B P P I.

First published by B P P I in June 2001 in *Plays By Frank Pugliese*

First edition, this book: August 2020
I S B N: 978-0-88145-785-8

Book design: Marie Donovan
Page make-up: Adobe InDesign
Typeface: Palatino

THE SUMMER WINDS was originally produced by Naked Angels, opening on 29 May 1991. The cast and creative contributors were:

LOUNGE SINGER............................Timothy Britten Parker
SAM..Jeff Williams
ANNE... Ashley Crow
JOE..Gareth Williams
MARY...Lisa Eichorn
RICK... Barry Sherman
JO..Kelly Wolf
LOU..Geoffrey Nauffts
JANIE... Marisa Tomei

Director..Gareth Williams
Set design.. Rick Sobel
Lighting design............................John-Paul Szczepanski
Casting...Brett Goldstein
Production stage manager............................... Jenny Peek

PRODUCTION NOTE

The play can be performed with two actors or eight. However many actors are used, each character in the play is different and the actor must change accordingly. The number of actors involved will dictate the production. Eight actors make for a festive occasion, while four will bring a lot of focus on the actors and the combinations the director uses them in. No matter how many actors are used it should be a celebration of the versatility and scope of theatre.

SETTING

Place—a lounge in Brooklyn.

Time—present. A summer night. The play begins as the sun goes down and ends as the sun comes up. If the director finds this important he can have the LOUNGE SINGER *deal with time as he announces the scenes.*

Set—the place is a down and out lounge in some motel or hotel in Brooklyn. One of those places that you stop in on the way to someplace else. Maybe you're fighting with a wife or a lover and you have to get a drink, and this is the only place around. And the singer has left his voice somewhere on the road. If he came from any other neighborhood but the one he came from, he'd be called the next Frank Sinatra. The play takes place in this lounge. The lounge, maybe with a chair or a booth, turns into a bedroom, or a living room, or a bar. The narrator will be singing about love. But what we see is, hopefully, the reality of love.

LOUNGE SINGER—*he is the narrator of the play. He's a second-rate singer who wants to be up there with Bobby Darrin and his hero Frank Sinatra. His fantasy is to one day play in a Las Vegas Hotel. He's played beat-up single's bars and smelly motel lounges his whole life, but he still maintains his style and sings. Even when he is sweating on this summer night he still smokes his cigarette, drinks his scotch and tries to stay cool. The songs are that collection all lounge singers sing from* The Summer Winds *to* Somewhere Beyond the Sea. *On stage he should play the audience as though he were in a real lounge, dedicating songs to women in the audience, striking up conversation with the audience and using them for his act. He should ad lib lines for laughs and the introductions. He should be directly involved with the audience as though it were a nightclub. He should try to talk about love, but only bitterness and regrets come up.*

(LOUNGE SINGER *is looking on the floor.*)

(*Lights come up.*)

(*He looks at the audience.*)

LOUNGE SINGER: Anybody see a money clip? ...Just the clip. I'm always losin', my home, my wife, my way.... Nice to be here.
No really, it's great to be here....
Well actually, I hate bein' here....
Why should I lie to you? I only lie to the people I love. I don't wanna be here. I wanna go home. But where is home? Does anybody know? Maybe home is twenty years ago, three rooms in Brooklyn, watching Trudy roll up her shirt and cool down under the fire hydrant spray. Sometimes you get on that bus to whereever the hell we go and you just don't get off...until you come back. Barkeep, my fuel!
(*Squinting to take a look at the audience*)
Well, good evening ladies and gentlemen. I'll give you the benefit of the doubt.... But who can really know how good an evening can be. Only that bastard time can tell.... This is my show, the Summer Winds. I'd say welcome, if I meant it, but my body just woke up and my head is still passed out. There's a plus to passing out; you don't have to get dressed when you wake up. You don't have to punctuate how short a day is. You can just let them blur into one short life!
Barkeep, my conscious is dry!
How are your rooms? Is there enough room for two? My room is fine once

I put the brooms in the hallway.
I hope my agent is in the audience. Because he's fired!
I usually don't work a room this small.... I usually
don't work.
I am an artist; not a side show freak! I'm not the
background to your midnight gropings. I'm trying to
tell you something....
Barkeep!
God, it's hot out there. My throat is as dry as a shot
glass on Sunday morning....
(Pause)
WHO THE FUCK DO I HAVE TO FUCK TO GET A
SCOTCH IN THIS HOTEL! This is in my contract!

*(A WAITER brings LOUNGE SINGER a scotch and whispers
in his ear.)*

LOUNGE SINGER: Motel, hotel, what's the difference?
They all have check-out times. They all look alike....
The faces even look alike. You, I've seen you in every
town in this country.

(To the rest of the audience.)

I'M A SINGER! I don't know if you caught my
previous engagement, the back of the Greyhound
bus....

(Takes a drink)

I sing love songs. I sing'em in the summer because
that's when people need'em the most. That's when
the love you plant in spring hits that high note like an
open rose. Or it dries out like a burnt piece of grass. On
this night that's hotter than the day it came from. On
a night when the air is dead silent. On a night where
the birds that whistle at sunrise decide to whistle
at sunset. Like some miracle I feel like a Greek god,
Mercury, like the F T D florist man, with wings on my
feet. And I'll blow through this city and my gift to you

and this lousy unforgiving world will be a moment of coolness....

(He sings a song.)

(The lights go down on the stage and come up on the bar area.)

(First Set—seated on a barstool is a man [SAM] in his early twenties. In walks a woman [ANNIE] in her early thirties; she sits down next to the man. Sinatra music fills the background.)

ANNIE: *(Looking up at the bar)* Gin and tonic. *(She begins to look for her money. She can't find it and gets nervous.)* I forgot my money...I'll be back in a second.

SAM: That's okay. It's on me.

ANNIE: Thanks. *(She stares at him and looks him over.)* Thank you.

SAM: It's okay.

(A pause as ANNIE and SAM each sip on their drinks.)

ANNIE: I can get you the money.

SAM: It's okay.

ANNIE: Take me a second.

SAM: Forget it.

(Another pause as ANNIE and SAM each continue to drink.)

SAM: You got the time...? I mean, you know what time it is?

ANNIE: Eleven thirty.

SAM: That's all?

ANNIE: That's all.

SAM: Empty.

ANNIE: I'm fine.

SAM: The place.

ANNIE: Oh yeah... This is always a bad night.

SAM: Come here often...? Excuse me, I mean do you come here a lot?

ANNIE: Not a lot. Enough, you can say.

SAM: New for me... Hot out there.

ANNIE: I needed a drink.... I was sweatin' real bad. Air conditioner's busted.

SAM: Don't got one... Noticed the green.

ANNIE: They just painted the outside.

SAM: Catches the eye.

ANNIE: I think it's tacky....

SAM: It made me pull over.

ANNIE: Thanks for the drink.

SAM: It's good to see somebody else in here, hate drinkin' alone.

ANNIE: I needed a drink after tonight.

SAM: You and me both. *(A pause)* Whatta you do?

ANNIE: Whatta you mean?

SAM: Whatta you do? Job or whatever?

ANNIE: Teach aerobics... But I'm a dancer.

SAM: Where do you teach it?

ANNIE: Gym uptown. In the City.

SAM: Keep your shape...I mean it keeps you healthy.

ANNIE: I guess I was an aerobic teacher I should say.

SAM: Are you just a dancer now?

ANNIE: My last day was today. They gave me a party.

SAM: Another job dancing?

ANNIE: I'm moving back home. Had it with the city.

SAM: Where's that?

ANNIE: Wichita, Kansas. Fast food capital of the world.

SAM: You were born there?

ANNIE: I'm just a lil' ole Kansas girl…. I wonder if I'll get the accent back. Ten years is a long time.

SAM: You gonna teach aerobics out there?

ANNIE: I don't know what I'm gonna do. Maybe I'll just take it easy for awhile.

SAM: You gonna dance?

ANNIE: No… I don't dance back there.

SAM: I always wanted to learn how to dance.

ANNIE: Take lessons.

SAM: It wouldn't make a difference, I got two left feet.

ANNIE: Anybody can dance. Just takes practice, lots of practice.

SAM: I can't dance. I mean I do a little two-step or something that moves. But dance like a dancer, no way.

ANNIE: What do you do?

SAM: Some people are actors who wait tables. I'm a waiter who acts.

ANNIE: You act?

SAM: Not really.

ANNIE: I'm an actor too. I take lessons. I really learned a lot. You know if only all the teachers in this city would act we'd have better stuff. I was just always taking lessons…I guess I should say I took lessons until two days ago.

SAM: I never really did any acting.

ANNIE: But you're an actor?

SAM: Well…yeah.

ANNIE: I sing too.

SAM: A triple threat.

ANNIE: Yeah, the triple threat of Wichita, Kansas.

SAM: You might say I'm a triple threat. I can't act, sing or dance. That's why I wanna be a director.

ANNIE: A director. You got a part for me? I really am a terrific actress if somebody would give me a chance.

SAM: Right now I'm just a stage manager at an Off Off Broadway play.

ANNIE: Where is it?

SAM: Well, it's so off it's in New Jersey…Hoboken. A couple a' blocks in.

ANNIE: A girl in my class lived there. She liked it alright.

SAM: It's alright…

ANNIE: It's been alright.

SAM: It's just, I was born in the city. Always been around the business so I always wanted to be a part of it. And it's always been a part of me.

ANNIE: But were you an actor?

SAM: I was an actor when I got out of school. But it doesn't take long to realize you're not an actor. It's crazy business.

ANNIE: I'll always be a dancer. Maybe not here, but I know I can dance… My husband is an actor… You have seen him. He's got a few commercials. Black curly hair, moustache, handsome.

SAM: You're married?

ANNIE: Was.

SAM: Oh… Sorry.

ANNIE: Don't be silly... It was years ago. He's from Kansas too. We came out here together. I was seventeen, dropped out of high school to be a star.... The bastard dumped me the first break he got.

SAM: Nice music.

(There is a long pause as ANNIE and SAM listen.)

SAM: It's crazy business, ain't it.

ANNIE: You smoke? *(She takes out a cigarette.)*

SAM: No.

ANNIE: You mind?

SAM: No, I like it.

ANNIE: I don't have to smoke.

SAM: It's okay.

ANNIE: Just tell me if it bothers you. *(She lights it and begins smoking it.)* I know it's pretty bad for you... And me being an exercise teacher and all...I figure I'm allowed one vice.

SAM: There's cancer everywhere.

ANNIE: Exactly. Just breathin' city air is worse than a pack a day. Midwest air is very clean.

SAM: My girlfriend smokes a lot.

ANNIE: *(Pause as she checks her watch)* What does she do?

SAM: She wants to be in movies.

ANNIE: As what?

SAM: As nothing. She just wants to be in 'em. Doesn't care where or how.

ANNIE: She get a lot of work?

SAM: I don't know, she's with her sister in L A. Haven't heard from her in a month.

ANNIE: Maybe she's busy.

SAM: She'll be back when her money runs out, but this time she'll be sorry. *(Pause)* What kind of music do you like?

ANNIE: All kinds. I like this place, they play the old guys...I like jazz.

SAM: I love jazz... What kind?

ANNIE: Saxophones and clarinet.

SAM: I mean like fusion or somethin' else?

ANNIE: I don't know the names. I played a lot of it, though, when I worked as a bartender.

SAM: I like Coltrane, always have, always will.

ANNIE: I got a friend helped write that song on the radio.

SAM: Which one?

ANNIE: The one about birds.

SAM: Really?

ANNIE: She gets three hundred grand a year for it.

SAM: For that song?

ANNIE: It's an okay song. It's just a love song.

SAM: Yeah, it's okay...three hundred thousand dollars is okay too.

ANNIE: You know it's nice to meet straight guys.

SAM: Must be a problem.

ANNIE: No kiddin'. They're either married or gay. Not that I have anything against either one, just a girl can't get a break in this city. I just don't meet nice guys.

SAM: How long you been here?

ANNIE: Ten aggravating years... You are straight, aren't you?

SAM: Yeah, I am.

ANNIE: You must have it easy. There isn't too many like you around.

SAM: It's hard to talk to people.

ANNIE: You're talkin' to me.

SAM: You have pretty eyes.

ANNIE: Thank you... They're my mom's.

SAM: They're yours and they look Italian.

ANNIE: My mom's Italian. My dad's Irish.

SAM: The best of both worlds.

ANNIE: Or the worst... But they're great. My dad teaches at Witchita State. *(She pauses for a moment.)* He teaches English...stuff like that. My mom's a physical therapist; very athletic. I take after her.

SAM: I'm Italian.

ANNIE: You don't look it.

SAM: Whatta I look?

ANNIE: French.

SAM: That's a new one...I'll take it as a compliment.

ANNIE: It's a compliment.

SAM: Thank you. *(Pause)* I like this old stuff... Hey, you wanna dance?

ANNIE: No thanks...I guess I should get going.

SAM: Why?

ANNIE: I still got packing to do.

SAM: I'll get you another drink.

ANNIE: Thanks...but really—

SAM: One more.

ANNIE: Make it a Coke. Maybe I'm gonna have to stay up.

SAM: A Coke.

ANNIE: I had a small, little going-away party with all my friends. They're really wonderful people. Really, I mean that... It was a dinner party, but they all had to leave early, work and stuff.

SAM: You get any good presents?

ANNIE: I got a big picture book of ballet.

SAM: That must be nice.

ANNIE: They don't understand.

SAM: What?

ANNIE: You know I've studied ballet since I was five.

SAM: You must be good.

ANNIE: Damn right I was good. I was a dancer... They operated on my knees six times... Damn, I got ugly knees.

SAM: I can't believe that.

ANNIE: I got scars all around them...you know they told me I wouldn't dance again. But I did, and good too... But the scars blow me jobs in Vegas and Atlantic City.

SAM: How about tights...I mean you could wear tights.

ANNIE: Almost got a job in Atlantic City. I had it; the girl they gave it to wasn't half as good as me...that job had tights, but who am I kiddin', ten years goin' at it? It just isn't going to happen. They don't give a shit for talent.

SAM: Why don't you teach? That might be nice.

ANNIE: I thought about it...maybe.

SAM: You could teach in Kansas, maybe.

ANNIE: Maybe...but they expected me to be a star, not a teacher.

SAM: My folks expected me to be a doctor, but I'm not. It's alright.

ANNIE: But I wanted to be a star.

SAM: Then don't give up.

ANNIE: I'm not giving up.

SAM: I didn't mean it like that.

ANNIE: I'm just going back to Kansas to rest up and think things over. You have to understand that's my home. I was raised there. My friends are still back there.

SAM: You have friends here, don't you?

ANNIE: Yeah, but they're not real friends. You understand. They're very nice, but they're like, you know, not real.

SAM: Insincere.

ANNIE: You could put it that way. I sorta feel empty in a real sorta sad way when I'm around them.

SAM: Let me tell you somethin'. Friends back home are no better.

ANNIE: It'll be nice sleeping in my old room.

SAM: Will you send me a postcard or somethin'?

ANNIE: Why sure... Here, let me have your address... You have a pen?

SAM: I got a pen. Here, I'll rip this card in half. *(He rips the business card in half and writes on one half, then hands over the cards and pen.)*

ANNIE: And here's mine... Send me a postcard of the Empire State Building.

SAM: Alright, that's a deal.

ANNIE: Thanks for the drinks.

SAM: You're not leaving yet?

ANNIE: I gotta get back to work.

SAM: Come on, stay… don't leave so fast.

ANNIE: I really should go. It was nice meeting you. *(She looks at the paper.)* Sam.

SAM: You can call me Sammy.

ANNIE: I didn't even introduce myself. I'm Anne Grice.

SAM: Glad to meet you, Miss Grice.

ANNIE: And I'm glad to meet you, Mr Pino.

SAM: You know, Anne, if I had someone to teach me dancing, I bet I could dance.

ANNIE: I know a great teacher. Her classes are cheap and she is a wonderful lady. Really one of the best. You want her number?

SAM: Would you like to dance, Anne, a nice slow one?

ANNIE: Would you like a cigarette? *(She lights another one.)*

SAM: No thank you…I'm sorry, okay?

ANNIE: I don't need to dance with you.

SAM: Maybe I need to dance with you… Maybe I would think of it as something sort of special to dance with you, a dancer.

ANNIE: I'm sorry. I just really don't wanna dance… there's a dance club down the block you can go to. You can find a girl there to dance with.

SAM: Do you wanna come?

ANNIE: No thanks… Look, I have to leave now.

SAM: Anne, I really like you.

ANNIE: You're a nice guy…don't try to come on to me.

SAM: No…I'm not coming on. I like you. You have black soft hair, big beautiful eyes and I can feel your heart, it's warm.

ANNIE: I like you too…big deal, you wanna marry me or something? *(She laughs.)*

SAM: I'd marry you.

ANNIE: You're a crazy one…I got a ten o'clock flight and I still got a shitload of packing to do.

SAM: Alright. So we won't get married tonight.

ANNIE: Don't kid around.

SAM: Alright, I won't kid around…but I don't think you should leave tomorrow.

ANNIE: Why?

SAM: Because this is just the tip of the iceberg of one of the sweetest and nicest men to come out of New York City.

ANNIE: Modest too… So you're a city boy, is that it?

SAM: I'm on top of the situation.

ANNIE: I bet.

SAM: You want another drink?

ANNIE: I'm not finished with my coke.

SAM: I mean another drink.

ANNIE: Maybe I do need another one.

SAM: Two more gin and tonics.

ANNIE: Do you wanna sleep with me?

SAM: I'm not very tired.

ANNIE: You know what I mean.

SAM: You wanna know the truth? I would love to, but if I don't, I don't mind. I like you, Anne.

ANNIE: I'm not one night stand material.

SAM: That's why I don't want you to leave tomorrow.

ANNIE: You can't do this to me. I spent six months hating the men I met so I can take that plane tomorrow. So don't do this to me.

SAM: It's just that when you spend years looking for someone special, then all of a sudden it feels right...

ANNIE: You must have girls all over you... How old are you?

SAM: It's not the years that matter.

ANNIE: How old are you?

SAM: Twenty-two.

ANNIE: I'm going to be twenty-eight soon... You are so young. I can't believe this.

SAM: You don't look twenty-eight and I don't look twenty-two. Does it bother you? What difference does it make?

ANNIE: It doesn't bother me.

SAM: Do you like me?

ANNIE: I said I like you.

SAM: Then don't go. Look, we're two beautiful people...I'm lonely Anne, terribly lonely.

ANNIE: Damn it, I have to go... You think I'm not lonely either?

SAM: Why do you have to go?

ANNIE: Ten years I've been here—ten years I've tried to make it and ten years I've been kicked in the shins. I'm tired of it... And I'm tired of men who fuck you and forget you.

SAM: I think you're beautiful.

(There is a pause as ANNIE and SAM stare at each other. She kisses him:)

ANNIE: Thank you...you have so much to look forward to. You'll find someone younger and nicer. You don't even know me.

SAM: Anne, I wanna....

ANNIE: What? Whatta you wanna?

SAM: Anne, dance with me.

ANNIE: If I dance with you, are you gonna let me go home to pack?

SAM: I promise.

(ANNIE *gets up.* SAM *gets up. They slowly begin to dance.*)

ANNIE: You really can't dance.

SAM: I like this music.

ANNIE: You're soft.

SAM: You too.

ANNIE: Your eyes are nice.

SAM: You too.

ANNIE: Hold me.

(SAM *puts his arms around* ANNIE, *they hug, stop dancing and kiss.*)

ANNIE: Damn you, I have a plane to catch.

SAM: I'll help you pack.

(The lights fade.)

(In the dark the LOUNGE SINGER *breathes into the mike.)*

(Lights come up.)

LOUNGE SINGER: That's what a dying man sounds like in his sleep.... My mother's dead. My father's dead. And I'm dyin' of a loneliness that spreads through you like death. What can I say? I'm sorry.... Sorry for shooting stars, for long train rides, for walks in the

rain, sorry for all the things that make you realize how alone you really are....
By the way, thing haven't worked out for me....
I didn't ask to be here.
I want to be there, anywhere but here.
How many of you in the audience have been in love? How many of you in the audience have been hurt by love? How many of you in the audience wish you were dead?!
(To a woman in the audience)
Hello morning. Hello sunshine. Hello bacon and eggs. How would you like to spend the night with a man who thinks too much...?
(He moves away.)
Think about it.
(He winks.)
I'll make you die twice.
(To the audience)
1976, one big birthday party for Uncle Sam. Las Vegas. Nevada. A young man from New Jersey, a man full of song is opening for the King.
But the King never showed.
And the show never shined.
It was downhill after that, in a car without brakes. And the radio didn't work. I didn't even sing at ballgames. Trudy made the ice and I made the drinks. We were on the road, the side of the road. Cheap motels, greasy spoons stirring bitter coffee. But that coffee tasted better than the cup of sadness Trudy gave me.... She took my money clip, just the money. With a thumb and a dream I followed that money to a Times Square hotel. Rates by the hour—but I didn't need much time. The room was empty, except for a piece of vinyl spinnin' like the hour hand on the clock of my life.... I stood

on the ledge. Too many sad stories above the saddest story of all.

New York City.

And a wind hit me, a summer wind. It blew pieces around, a letter, a newspaper clipping, a photo taken in a Woolworth booth. It picks the pieces up and tosses them in your face. It'll force you to look at the pages of your life. We come in twos. I mean, any way you look at it we fit together. People weren't meant to be by themselves. If they were, God, that big piano player in the sky, woulda worked it out that way. When you stand on a ledge, you see that concrete city dressed up like a big birthday. And just as I tried to blow the candles out, I heard a song playin' from Trudy's empty room.... It went a little bit like this....

(Lights come up on a man sitting in the audience.)

(The LOUNGE SINGER *sings a song.)*

*(Second Set—the lights reveal a bedroom. Sitting is the man [*JOE*] eating cherries. Sitting on the bed is a woman [*MARY*] getting ready for bed.)*

MARY: You going to get into bed?

JOE: Second.

MARY: You still eating those things?

JOE: This is the best year for cherries since I been a kid. I just feel like eating them till I burst.

MARY: You're gonna get the runs. You know how you are with cherries.

JOE: You wanna watch some T V?

MARY: Not really. Do you?

JOE: No, not really.

MARY: Where are you putting those pits?

JOE: In my hand.

MARY: Don't touch anything until you wash 'em. You already ruined one set of sheets, I don't want another one streaked.

JOE: *(Gets up and goes to the window)* Remember the cherry tree we had in the backyard...? Black cherries almost as big as these... You think I should pull out the stump and put in another one? It was nice when it blossomed, wasn't it?

MARY: Why not pull it out? What's it doing back there anyway?

JOE: Looks good, though, where the lightning hit it. All split and burnt up like that—it was pretty... Mary, you think I planted enough flowers back there?

MARY: Joe, I don't think there's an inch you missed.

JOE: It'll look beautiful come spring... You happy in this house?

MARY: Bathrooms making funny noises again. I put on the shower and only hot would come on. Then I put on the sink and only cold comes out. How do you figure that?

JOE: Maybe I used up too much water pressure when I watered the yard.

MARY: You don't have to water it so much. They'll die again.

JOE: *(Pauses)* He's really going, isn't he?

MARY: Your brother can't sit still. He always knew what he wanted to do.

JOE: He won't write.

MARY: He said he would.

JOE: I know what he said, but he won't write. I raised him, I know.

MARY: Katy was sad, I could tell.

JOE: Want a cherry?

MARY: No, thank you... I think she was counting on marrying him...I guess she'll have to wait.

JOE: Germany... He won't be able to grow anything out there.

MARY: Germany's just a country, like any other.

JOE: I'm tellin' you cherries don't grow in Germany; Italy, yes. But Germany? Dad told us nothing grows in Germany since the war.

MARY: Sounds like our backyard.

JOE: I tell ya, when me and him were kids we'd grow tomato plants as tall as you. We got pictures of me and dad pickin' tomatoes the size of softballs.

MARY: Uncle Joe growing anything at the old house?

JOE: Nothin'... He's talkin' about sellin' the house. He was gonna give it to Tony and Katy, but now with Tony leavin', it's just him. He can't afford it.

MARY: I wish I could afford it.

JOE: He's dying... I see it in the cracks in his face. I feel bad for him. When mom died he gave up all he had and moved in with us. When dad died... Wish I could help him now.

MARY: We got money spread around.

JOE: I hope he gets to die in the house.

MARY: That's a depressing thought.

JOE: It's his place... I'd bury him in the yard.

MARY: He should come over more often. He can sit around in the backyard.

JOE: I tell you what, if the tomatoes grow like I plan, we'll get him a lawn chair and sit him right out there.

MARY: Then he isn't ever goin' to sit out there. You water them too much. You gotta leave 'em alone a little.

JOE: There's something wrong with that dirt. Maybe it needs some topsoil. The fertilizer doesn't seem to work at all.

MARY: You know Tony isn't the only one leaving. My cousin Suzanne is moving back out West, back with the family.

JOE: How's your mother feeling?

MARY: Still hurts a little, but she sounded okay on the phone... Can you stop eating those cherries? You're gonna get sick.

JOE: *(Puts the cherries down by the window and sits on the front of the bed)* I wonder what's on the—?

MARY: —Jesus Joe, you streaked the sheets again.

JOE: Shit. I wasn't thinking.

MARY: Goddamn it Joe, think a little.

JOE: It's alright, we'll get another sheet.

MARY: You just can't keep getting things.

JOE: I'm doing okay. With overtime I clear nine twenty... Mary, I been working day and night since I was twelve years old—I'm tired.

MARY: Sheets were made to last. We don't keep 'em more than a week before you get some shit on 'em.

JOE: Remember when I worked the jobs to get the down payment for the house? We figured it was all gonna be easy after that.

MARY: Joe, you always gotta make ends meet—it ain't never easy. *(She tries to clean the streak.)*

JOE: Let me ask you something. When we bought the house three years ago, did you know how bad the plumbing was?

MARY: No...I remember the roof needed patching, but I don't remember the plumbing.

JOE: Most of maintenance goes into plumbing. We spent a lot on the plumbing in this house.

MARY: Every house has got something wrong with it.

JOE: Maybe it's the pipes that are doing something to the water, that is doing something to the plants back there.

MARY: Could be. You mean rust and stuff?

JOE: Yeah, yeah, rust...you think rust could kill plants?

MARY: Could be.

JOE: You think rust water killed him?

MARY: Oh Joe, please, I don't wanna talk about it. I'll just cry again.

JOE: No, we don't have to talk about it. I just mean do you think drinking rusty water could've killed him?

MARY: Please.

JOE: Maybe you drinkin' the rusty water...

MARY: Alright enough already. I'm not gonna torture myself with that shit again.

JOE: I didn't even get to see him alive. They wouldn't even let me.

MARY: We'll have another one.

JOE: *(Goes back and has a cherry)* You sure you don't want one? They're really delicious. Sweet, hard, good cherry.

MARY: Your hand.

JOE: *(Wipes it on his pants)* See, clean.

MARY: Just get another pair of pants, right?

JOE: Mary, it's not important.

MARY: Pants and sheets are important to me, and if you think they're cheap, well…

JOE: Mary, I work so hard, I try to do the right thing, why does everything around me die? Five years ago when we were married we had a reception full of people, friends, family. Half of them are gone, and I don't see any of the guys anymore. I always got somethin' to do—broken fence, leaky roof, you name it… It's all dead or dying.

MARY: The doctor said there was nothing to do. He was stillborn. It's God, God, that's all.

JOE: Fuck 'em, that's all I have to say… He thinks Germany is any better? Well, fuck 'em.

MARY: He came here tonight to say goodbye and get your blessings, but you have to be nasty… You didn't even look him in the face when you spoke to him. What's a matter?

JOE: Whose gonna take care of Uncle Joe? I work, you work.

MARY: He's got a life too.

JOE: But the house.

MARY: It's just a house.

JOE: They'll sell the house.

MARY: You got your own house.

JOE: When I was ten my father took me into the basement and showed me this little room, and laid out inside was this train track that went in and out of the walls. It had mountains and a station… It was his when he was a kid. He showed it to me and didn't say a word. But I understood, it was mine.

MARY: You can put the trains in the basement.

JOE: The room, Mary...the room was mine—the wood paneling, the stone floor, the holes the trains come in and out of.

MARY: So whatta you wanna do about it? You wanna sell this house and buy that one? In a neighborhood where they rob the breath you breathe... Just get your uncle out of there. I don't blame your brother for leaving.

JOE: But Germany.

MARY: It's a great job. In a year he'll send over for Katy and he'll be fine.

JOE: How the hell am I supposed to afford seeing him?

MARY: You'll find a way.

JOE: I got this house to pay for...the bills, insurance.

MARY: We'll make it. We always do.

JOE: I don't know anymore. Is this it? Is this house it? All I worked for?

MARY: You want to still be living in three rooms over a laundromat? Living like a bum, working downstairs for minimum wage?

JOE: So now I'm better because I use a power tool? It's still dirt work.

MARY: What's a matter Joe? Why do we always disagree about everything?

JOE: I don't know.

MARY: Whatta you mean you don't know?

JOE: I mean I don't know.

MARY: I love you Joe...I still wait for you to come home for dinner and I still watch your face when you sleep.

JOE: Do I look old?

MARY: We're young. We got a lot of years ahead of us.

JOE: Sometimes I feel old. I feel the squeak in my joints and it hurts like I'm fallin' to pieces.

MARY: Damn it, you're so young and you talk like you're about to be dead and buried.

JOE: I feel dead.

MARY: When we first got married we ran around all over the place—the City, movies, friends. Now you come home and sleep.

JOE: I'm tired.

MARY: It isn't time to be tired. We gotta go out more.

JOE: Do you masturbate?

MARY: Come on, Joe.

JOE: Come on, tell me. I'm your husband. Do you masturbate?

MARY: Sometimes.

JOE: In the day?

MARY: Yeah, sometimes when I take a bath.

JOE: Whatta you think about?

MARY: I think about you.

JOE: Now let's be honest. Whatta you think about?

MARY: Situations, places. Hospitals, department stores… This is silly.

JOE: You think of other men?

MARY: Of course not. I think about you.

JOE: Mary, six years, you think about me?

MARY: Well…

JOE: Come on, honest.

MARY: Movie stars sometimes, or handsome men I see.

JOE: My brother. You ever masturbate with him?

MARY: Damn it, Joe, what is your problem? Of course not.

JOE: I masturbate with Katy. I masturbate with every woman I meet.

MARY: Am I that bad?

JOE: Mary, come on, we have good sex.

MARY: When we have it.

JOE: We're married.

MARY: We haven't fucked in weeks. I don't know how you expect to get a kid like that.

JOE: I'm not finished. Mary, sometimes I masturbate and think of prostitutes, with bodies and skin-tight clothes and....

MARY: Well, I guess a lot of men think about that.

JOE: Maybe, but lately I think about it all the time.

MARY: —Okay. I just don't want to hear about it. Okay?

JOE: *(Goes to the cherries)* Her lips were this color. *(He squeezes a cherry between his fingers.)*

MARY: Do all your fantasies have fruit in them?

JOE: Mary, two weeks ago I drove through the tunnel, to forty-fourth and twelfth and I stopped my car. And girls I masturbate with came up to the car and offered themselves to me for money. And I saw one with lips like this and.... And I opened the door without thinking and she came in. *(He sits in his chair.)* We drove to a rotted pier and I...in the car. And I kept thinkin' about you and me in high school and—

(MARY *smacks* JOE.)

MARY: Don't compare me to a whore...you pig. *(She gets up and goes to the window.)*

JOE: I went back there three times for her, and three times we went to the pier. I thought about the pier fallin' and throwing me into the river. I wished it would.

MARY: I can smell it... So what? You have a disease or something? Why the hell are you telling me this?

JOE: I just don't know why I went. I hate it, but I kept going back.

MARY: You don't hate it.

JOE: Mary, I'm sorry.

MARY: Sorry for what?

JOE: For this.

MARY: For the plumbing, for the house, for the stinkin' whore... Maybe it was too much to ask to be faithful. But we can forgive. Don't go back... Damn you, Joe! I just can't have you walking around here like the walking dead or somethin'. I want you back. I don't see you anymore. I really don't know who you are sometimes...anymore.

JOE: Whatta we gonna do Mary? Six years ago it all looked so simple, so pretty. Then the house—I really loved it Mary. It was bright, now it's dying.

MARY: *(She pauses as she stares out the window.)* ...Maybe this year we'll eat a salad from the backyard.

JOE: Do you feel bad about the kid?

MARY: Is it the kid? Do you hate me? Do you blame me for killing the kid?

JOE: No, Mary—that's what I wanted to say. I don't blame you. I blame myself for killing things. I want to kill myself.

MARY: Joe, I love you. Believe this or don't.

JOE: I don't know what it is, but I feel numb and tired inside. Cold… It started happening a couple of months ago. Nothing makes sense. We'd fuck and your face was…. I mean, you would orgasm and I would think, I've never seen this face before.

MARY: They say, they're all the same. My mother told me. I said, "Not Joe, he loves me like a lover, not a husband."

JOE: You're all I have, Mary. My friends are gone, my brother is gone, my uncle is dying. And the old house is dead.

MARY: Joe, you think I have anybody else?

JOE: Sometimes I'm so lonely, I walk in the backyard and think about you and I wonder what I'm doing.

MARY: And?

JOE: I don't know anymore.

MARY: Maybe it's just a phase, Joe… Do you like me?

JOE: I like you Mary. You're my friend. We don't fight much, do we?

MARY: We don't. We get along okay.

(JOE *stares at* MARY *for a moment.*)

JOE: But I don't feel love anymore. It's killing me, but I'm just empty… You want me to leave? I'll go to my uncle's.

MARY: Do you want to leave?

JOE: Do you want me here? If you know I can't love you, can you have me here?

MARY: Maybe you should go.

JOE: *(Begins to put his clothes on)* Whatta you going to do if I leave?

MARY: I don't know, Joe...I feel like crying.

JOE: I will still help you out with the house, you know that.

MARY: It's a big house.

JOE: I'm sorry Mary, I wanted it to work, I did.

MARY: Please leave. I really want to cry now.

JOE: *(He is dressed.)* Bye.

MARY: Your cherries.

JOE: You want 'em?

MARY: Take 'em.

JOE: *(He goes to the cherries.)* Do you want me to go?

MARY: Do you want to go?

JOE: I don't know where to go. The old man won't handle it—my brother...I mean, this is my house.

MARY: But do you want to go?

JOE: I don't know... What if I stay?

MARY: Do you want to stay? It's up to you—you can stay or go. Whatever you want to do.

(They stare at each other for a while. JOE *slowly takes off his clothes again. He is left in his pajama pants.)*

MARY: Quiet Joe...

JOE: I'm so scared.

MARY: We'll go get a tree in the morning....

(The lights fade as MARY *begins to cry as they lie still.)*

(The LOUNGE SINGER *takes a drink.)*

LOUNGE SINGER: The bootleggers in this gin joint, who water this piss down, want me to stick to the songs.... Well, these songs are stuck to me like a band-aid over a bullet hole shot from the gun they call LOVE!

(To management)
You can't play me like a juke box in a run-down diner.
You can't drop quarters into the slits they call my eyes!
The words in these songs are like nails....
Like the nails they'll hammer into the lid of my coffin.
You want me to sing?!
You want a love song?!
You want a punch in the eye?!
(He breaks down into tears. The tears turn into laughter.)
I been in show business so long I'm like a two-bit actor who doesn't know the difference between laughing and crying.
Why do I kill myself every night?
Why do I squeeze my head like a bar keep's lemon?
Why do my tears taste like cheap bourbon?
To the barkeep, the anesthesiologist of my soul.
God bless you.
Until last call you're the only man I trust in Coney Island.
WAITER: Canarsie!
LOUNGE SINGER: My home.... "Can I see?" I can see I'm dyin' out here.
I'll never forget my eighth grade teacher, Mr Fleishman, that's right, like the margarine. Like the margarine they use to fry the burger they call my brain —He told me, before he kicked me outa school and into life. "Why do you sing this shit, you two-bit punk?"
He was my mentor.
I sing for Trudy.
For the guys on Cropsey Avenue, drinkin booze, pitchin' pennies, goin' nowhere....
Ah, to go back to nowhere.

They called me the next Domenico Modugno. But when you come from the same street as the Chairman of the Board, that's not so great.

Some nights, when my sheets are soaked with yesterday's goodbyes, I think of Trudy. Maybe one night she'll hear me stretch my cords. She'll hear me squeek my pitch. She'll hear the hurt you call music.

(Looks into the audience)

.Trudy...?

Oh God, in that great big gig they call heaven. Thank you!

My eighty-proof prayer has been answered.

Ladies and Gentlemen, Trudy's here.

Trudy, baby, I waited, twenty years I waited like a dog in the rain.

Trudy.

Trudy.

Trudy.

(A man throws a drink in his face.)

LOUNGE SINGER: Mister, I'm so sorry.

Barkeep! I'm comin' too!

(To the audience)

You, the happy ones, do you know what it's like to be me?

No one falls in love with greasy hair.

No one falls for a guy who lives out of a shopping bag. All that Trudy left me was an empty bottle and I moved in.

It's a funny thing standin' on a ledge. Your mistakes get as clear as gin.

My advice? Make it special. Try to make it special. You know what people die of? Boredom. Boredom sets in your bones and bang, you're gonna get a heart attack of cancer, or like walk in front of a bus?

Don't rely on the past. The past can get you like a drunken hit and run.

To Trudy, wherever you are, a song.

(A song)

(The song becomes distant, as though we can hear it through the wall as the light come up on the....)

(Third Set—a motel room. There is a bed, a night table, a window with the shades closed. The hum of an air conditioner fills the background. The sheets are thrown off. Face-down left is a naked woman [JO] watching the air conditioner. To the right is a naked man [RICK] laying on his back. He turns slowly to the night table and gets a stick of gum and puts it in his mouth.)

JO: Wish I had an air conditioner... It's been murder lately. I been gettin' dizzy sometimes.

RICK: It's summer...it's hot.

JO: You must be used to it.

RICK: I don't think about it much. *(He pulls out a cigarette and lights it. He blows the smoke over his body.)* There's a pool of sweat laying between my chest. I can feel the chill drilling through me.

(RICK blows smoke over himself again. JO turns her head and puts her hand on his chest and rubs it gently.)

JO: That feel better...? Warm ya' up? Heat ya' up?

RICK: Chill splitting me in half. *(He blows smoke over himself again.)*

JO: Whatta ya' doin' that for?

RICK: Warm me up.

JO: I'll warm you up.

(JO pulls herself on RICK and begins to kiss his chest.)

RICK: *(He puts his hand on her head.)* Your hair.

JO: I missed ya'. ...I hated ya and missed ya at the same time.

RICK: Your hair is shorter.

JO: What ya' think when ya' saw me?

RICK: Your hair was shorter.

JO: When I seen you there, I coulda dropped. Sittin' by yourself on Charlie's stoop. Lickin' your ice cream all cool and slow. It was like you were waitin' for the boys. It was like a picture from high school.

RICK: It was hot.

JO: Almost as hot as tonight.

RICK: Almost.

JO: What ya think when ya saw me?

RICK: I told you. Your hair looked shorter. But when you smiled it was like I never left. I guess it was strange.

JO: Why?

RICK: You like the restaurant?

JO: It's funny, I didn't think anybody really smoked after fuckin'.

RICK: I like cliches.

JO: Cliches? *(Pause)* You chewin' gum too, like ya used to.

RICK: Gets the taste out.

JO: Of me? Fuckin'?!

RICK: The restaurant. The food was plain awful.

JO: I liked it. It was romantic... I ain't had romantic for a long time.

RICK: I don't know the new yuppy places up there. We still got yuppies? Looked nice from the outside.

JO: I just wanted to be sure.

RICK: I know. Look, I didn't want a scene either.

JO: He's got friends all over.

RICK: It's okay.

JO: It was nice to come back here. Remember prom night, Rick? I swear to you it was the nicest night I had, maybe in my life. We were somethin' back then. All them kids hangin' around us like that. We was hot, wasn't we?

RICK: You was hot. I was lukewarm.

JO: I was hot, wasn't I? Good lookin' too. After the kid, I just couldn't lose it. I look fat, don't I?

RICK: You look older.

JO: *(She looks at her hand.)* I used to have cute little fingers. Now they're fat.

RICK: They're still you. You filled in a little, that's all.

JO: Thank you.

RICK: You still look good.

JO: Thanks, Rick—what we do that night?

RICK: Dancing.

JO: At that night club, right?

RICK: The ferry. Chinese food. ...Then back here.

JO: It was so nice, that night. I remember wakin' up and watchin' the light shoot in through the curtains. A slice of it cuttin' across the room. I turned over and saw your face on the pillow. You were so cute, Rick. I kissed you. Remember I started kissin' you and we made love again while the light was shootin' in? I don't forget that, I don't forget.

RICK: It looked orange to me, the whole night... This room used to be orange. They changed it, didn't they?

JO: We had breakfast on the beach. Then you took me home. Ya' know after that night I would dream of Sheepshead Bay like it was some tropic island...I was hurt.

RICK: I came back. *(He goes to the window.)* Too cold for you in here. I'm gonna lower this a little.

JO: *(Pulls the sheets up)* It's alright, leave it alone. I could use a little cold. Gets any hotter I'm gonna melt.

RICK: I went to school.

JO: I know where you went, but why?

RICK: To learn.

(JO picks up a bottle of scotch and drinks it.)

RICK: Since when do you drink after fuckin'?

JO: Five years is a long time.

RICK: Five years is long or short, depends how you look at it.

JO: Any way I look at it, it's five years.

RICK: We were kids.

JO: Now we ain't.

RICK: How much you drink?

JO: Just enough and not too much.

(RICK lets out a small laugh.)

JO: Whatta you laughin' at?

RICK: Cliches. *(He puts his face into the air conditioner.)*

JO: You'll get sick like that.

RICK: Cold makes me tired. How was winter?

JO: Not too bad.

RICK: I never finished...I never finished school. Two years and I left. Banged around out there. Small jobs and stuff... Like I said, I like cliches... They're proven.

JO: Two letters the first year and then nothin'...I woulda waited....

RICK: That's why I stopped writing.

JO: I was pissed.

RICK: When'd you marry him?

JO: Three years ago. You know him don't you?

RICK: I don't want to run into him.

JO: Sometimes when he was layin' on me, I'd be thinkin about you. And I say that's sick, it's sick Joanne. Don't think that shit or you ain't never gonna come. But I keep thinkin' it. And the more I don't wanna think it, the more I think it. He ain't around much, he's on the road....

RICK: We could drink and smoke.

JO: We could.

RICK: You ever been to New Mexico?

JO: You know I ain't never been to New Mexico.

RICK: Five years ain't such a long time.

JO: What's in New Mexico?

RICK: Dirt that's sweet when you taste it... Red dirt that tastes sweet when you taste it. You wanna go to New Mexico?

JO: Must be hot in New Mexico.

RICK: It's hot.

JO: Hotter than this?

RICK: Almost. I got a house in New Mexico. An empty house as big as this room. And it's made of red dirt. And in the summer it gets so hot in there, you can bake bread.

JO: Don't it got windows?

RICK: Keep 'em closed or else the coyotes eat the bread.

JO: Sounds miserable.

RICK: It is miserable.

JO: Why don't you sell it?

RICK: People and promise still live there.

JO: I thought it was empty.

RICK: There's a lot of ways to be empty.

JO: Don't make fun of me.

RICK: How old is your kid?

JO: Two... Oh, he's a little brat.

RICK: Kids don't belong in New Mexico, it's too hot... Heat's enough to kill you in New Mexico.

JO: Are you alright? You keep sayin' New Mexico.

RICK: Not too much grows there. The sun makes it sprout really fast and then it burns it up.

JO: How about California?

RICK: You wanna go to California?

JO: Must be nice.

RICK: California has a lot of beaches. More than Brooklyn. You'd love it.

JO: You're makin' fun of me.

RICK: *(He goes to the bed and hugs her.)* I'm sorry. I have no excuses and my explanation doesn't explain much.

JO: I called up your house and your mom says you're in California. I was hurt. I was hurt bad. I couldn't care if you lived or died.

RICK: Does he work a lot?

JO: Ya didn't even tell me you were leaving.

RICK: Does he drive out to California?

JO: Sometimes.

RICK: You ever go with him, places, and do stuff.

JO: That's not fair.

RICK: I always wanted to drive a truck.

JO: I don't love him, if that's what you're talkin' about. I hate him. I can't stand his face sometimes.

RICK: Don't lie to me Joanne.

JO: I don't love him.

RICK: You don't have to love him to be married to him.

JO: I loved you.

RICK: And I loved you. *(He goes back to the window.)*

RICK: Should I open the shades?

JO: What for?

RICK: The City looks somethin' tonight. I missed the City.

JO: How about California, ain't they got cities?

RICK: I missed this city. And my whole life I been goin' the other way. Let's go in.

JO: I have to leave in a little.

RICK: Why?

JO: The kid's at my mothers and I'm at my sister's.

RICK: Stay the night.

JO: My mother has the kid and my sister don't stay out all night.

RICK: Sky's clear and the water is calm. I can't even notice how hot it is out there from here. Don't know if it's summer or winter.

JO: Whatya study?

RICK: Nothing important. I need a drink. *(He throws out the gum, pours some scotch in his glass and lights another cigarette. He sits in a chair.)*

JO: So tell me what else happened? Five years is a long time.

RICK: Nothing much happened. You wanna watch T V?

JO: No, not really.

RICK: What happened to you?

JO: Boring. I got marred and got a kid. You know it all.

RICK: Yeah, boring. Do you think I drink a lot?

JO: No...well...maybe...I don't know. Yeah.

RICK: I don't. I drink very little. Never drank very much... How many drinks did I have prom night?

JO: I don't remember.

RICK: Six, six drinks. I remember it exactly. The next day I was so sick I couldn't even walk. I threw up the whole day. I was still sick all the way into graduation.

JO: You looked nice graduation. That was a beautiful suit. I still have the pictures. He hates when I look at'em. He screams and does stupid things.

RICK: He was always like that. They pinched hit for him at the Trenton game and he busted a bat on the side of the dugout. He struck out three times that day.

JO: Homecoming, you and me danced up a storm. We were amazing. You still got the yearbook with our picture in it.

RICK: What picture?

JO: You don't remember? It's got you and me dancing and it says underneath, "may all their nights be like this".

RICK: I don't remember.

JO: Mr Sherwood wrote it. He even had poetry written up in a magazine once. He liked you and me, he said it was romantic.

RICK: Mr Sherwood is romantic. *(He goes to the window.)*

JO: What's a matter Rick? I still know you. I can still feel you.

RICK: That restaurant was awful. I been spitting up the taste of that place all night. The chicken tasted like it was pickled in something. Don't you agree?

JO: I liked it; it was fun. We talked about old times. We held hands. I liked it Rick.

RICK: Old times. The past. I can't believe Charlie's in prison.

JO: Cocaine.

RICK: I wanted to see him.

JO: You can visit him.

RICK: I wouldn't do that to him. Spoil the memory.

JO: *(She gets up and hugs him.)* All these years I put you out. Then you show up with your fuckin' ice cream cone melting all over your hand. And you're licking it, trying not to let it all melt. I saw you then and… My life is not what I thought it was gonna be.

RICK: Whatta we do? Wait till he drives away. Lock ourselves up in hotel rooms and drink, smoke, and fuck ourselves into memory.

JO: I'll leave him.

RICK: And you'll come to me.

JO: Yes.

RICK: You don't belong in New Mexico.

JO: We can stay here.

RICK: It's a small room.

JO: It seemed so special then.

RICK: I have promises left out there.

JO: How about the promises you made me?

RICK: Now we both sound like cliches... *(He kisses her.)* It's getting late.

JO: *(She goes back to the bed.)* Let's make love again, before I have to leave.

RICK: Yeah. Let me finish this cigarette.

(JO *drinks some scotch and then stares at the ceiling.*)

JO: Funny ceiling...

(RICK *opens the window.*)

JO: What ya' opening the window for?

RICK: Let some heat in, it's getting cold.

JO: Get into bed.

(RICK *slowly turns from the window.*)

RICK: Once, Charlie and me we were playin' stickball at the schoolyard. It was summer and I was gettin' tired. He was hitting me all over, and each pitch got me more tired. Then finally I let one just sail in, he smacked it over the fence and into this ditch they dug out to build one a the projects. I climbed the fence. And there was a demolished house, everywhere. And piles of sand, and dirt. Rubble everywhere. So on a pile of dirt, I see the ball. So I go over, climb up and grab it. When I see a couple of hairs sticking out of the dirt. So I don't know why, but I dig a little and out comes this head. A beautiful girl with long blonde hair. I touched her face and it's flab, like it's dead, a little cold, but still a little hot from the sun. So I call Charlie over and we dig out some more, and we see where she is cut up. She's cut up all over. She was naked. I never saw a naked girl before, a live one...I mean. —And she was dead, with crusted blood all over her and holes of flesh. Charlie touched her, then I did… We looked around and ran, till we flagged a cop car down on the corner. Flashing lights, some kinda car from the morgue. They asked us some questions and let us go. She was a girl from the neighborhood. I remembered her because she had big tits…I never forgot that. We started going together a little while after… But Joanne, I'll never forget her face.

JO: Can't you remember the good times?

RICK: What?

JO: The good times.

RICK: *(He goes and sits next to here in bed.)* Yeah, the good times.

(RICK puts the cigarette out with his foot. The lights fade.)

LOUNGE SINGER: Richard Rogers, dead. Cole Porter, dead. Irving Berlin—

(The theater goes in the dark.)

LOUNGE SINGER: —WOW! Am I out?
That's a first.
The club blacked out before I did….
Is this me?

(The MANAGER goes up to LOUNGE SINGER on stage.)

LOUNGE SINGER: What?
You got to be kidding me.
(He turns, he flashes a flashlight on himself.)
Don't worry, it's still me. I'm still here. I always be here. I was born here.
I'll probably die here. If I haven't already.
(To the band)
Why don't you rub two drum sticks together and start a fire.
At least we'd see somethin'….

Nice rubbin', nice rubbin'.
(To the audience)
This place wouldn't be hot if it was burnin' down....
It sure is dark. It reminds me of the dark ages, or the last fifteen of my life. My voice ran away from me, and I couldn't find it. Actually, I think I found somebody else's voice.
In a glass.
On the rocks.
Watered down.
(Still dark)
In this kinda light, she always looks good. She, I mean she's, I mean she's, I need a break. We all look good in the dark. With the lights out, you're a good-lookin' crowd.
(Points the light at the audience)
And easy on the eyes. Easy on the eyes. Ice. Eyes.
Can I get a light?
...God, doesn't that sound like my life.
Maybe the whole state's blacked out. Maybe I'm still sleepin'?
Hey, what's everybody doin' in my room?
Can't be. I usually have to pay to get people in my room.
(The spotlight is back on. It's not on Pinky. Pinky runs towards the light. The light goes to where Pinky was. They criss-cross in this fashion another two times.)

(Pointing at the spotlight operator)

LOUNGE SINGER: Barkeep! I want whatever he's drinkin'!

(Pinky fakes to move and then stands still. The light is on him. He wipes the sweat from his brow.)

LOUNGE SINGER: Gotya! Either I'm getting slower, or that light is gettin' smarter.

I'm always tryin' to get into the light. Last time I got into a bright light...
The bus hit me.
The only red light I stop for is in a window.
Sure I drink and drive.
What am I gonna do? Stop drivin'?
Yeah, I get into accidents. That's how I meet people.
Can I get a little help from my friends? No, this is not a segue. My friend, Johnny Walker. Frustration, he's here.
Disappointed and despair, they always come to my show. But my friends, they cost me.

(*A* WAITER *brings* LOUNGE SINGER *a drink; he looks at it.*)

LOUNGE SINGER: I said, easy on the ice! (*He pours it down.*) This is that time in the show when we open up. Hey, where you goin'?!
I said open up, not close down.
This is the time in the show, when we include you the audience. Rich or poor. I owe you. I'm in debt. Whatever I got in this big blue teardrop of a world I owe to you people brave enough to come in here and have a drink, a laugh, and maybe a thought....
I owe you a piece of my bitter heart, sprinkled with arsenic.
'Cause that's the way I ate it.
So, any questions?
People really enjoyed this.... Once.
Right off the bat
...The bat they use to hit the baseball that is my head...
Don't ask me about the meaning of life.
The meaning of love.
The meaning of death.
Don't ask me about any four-letter words, they all mean the same to me.

I just sing'em…. I stopped hearin'em a long time ago.
(He points the mike at the audience.)
After doin' this for forever and a day
I know what you wanna ask, Pinky. And only my good friends call me Pinky… So, basically no one calls me Pinky.
(To the MANAGER*)*
Mr Pinky to you!
Where you been, Pinky?
You look bad, Pinky.
You got a dream, Pinky?!
What happen to your car, Pinky?!
What happen to the hundred bucks you owe me Pinky!?
I'm gonna answer all your questions tonight.
I been everywhere and nowhere, I feel bad too, they repossessed it and,
I AIN'T GOT A HUNDRED BUCKS!!!
Don't dreams come in your sleep…? I been awake a long time.
I want a place my own. And I ain't talking about the back row of the bus.
I'd call it Pinky's. Yeah, yeah, but no one else could call it Pinky's. Unless they're my friend… They'll have to call it, little finger's…ah, I don't care what they call it, as long as they pay to get in.
Pay to get in. Pay to get out. Whatever, I just know they're all gonna have
ta pay.
Everyone's got their own place.
Sinatra has his own place.
Nixon has his own place.
Next thing you know Harry Connick Junior is gonna have his own place. What's Harry Connick Junior got that I ain't got?

WAITER: Fans!

LOUNGE SINGER: Fans, air conditioners, what's the difference? When you're hot you're hot... This taste like—
—Like poison.
I was full of young, of bing, of bang, of boom. All I needed was a shot! POW!
I got shot in the head.
Trudy said, Pinky, you're too small for me!
I wanted to be a great man for Trudy. Not a scientist, or a tycoon, or a politician.... But a regular Joe. A guy you can call up and say, "Hey Joe, howya doin'?"
I woulda changed my name to Joe for Trudy.
A man dripping with character. Instead I'm dripping with, well I'm dripping.
Ah Trudy, you called me a jerk, you called me a fool, you called me a dope, but what you never called me... well you never called me back!
My only friend is a love song. They stood by me like beat-up crutches.
I love you, love song. You're pretty...
Pretty depressing.
I sing a love song like it's the last song I'll ever sing.
I'm just a satellite of this world. I'm gonna fly outa this nest they call a hotel room. With my wings of wax.
And as I hit the sun, they will melt. But a song will hit me like a big rush of wind. And it will lift me. And carry me out.
(To the piano player, as he plays)
Floyd, you're a, you're a...you're a piano player.

(A song... Then the LOUNGE SINGER *blows into his mic like he is the wind)*

(*Fourth Set—a subway station. Seated on a bench is a man* [LOU]. *Standing up looking for a train is a Hispanic woman* [JANIE].)

JANIE: There's a breeze when ya look for the train.

LOU: It's usually cool around this time.

JANIE: This summer has got to be one of the worst.

LOU: Every summer is bad... These pits don't make it no better.

JANIE: When I was a day lady it was cool... The air conditioner...you know.

LOU: Well the air conditioner, it's usually on. Cheaper to keep it going than to shut it off. But they were working on it tonight, ya hear the noise?

JANIE: Thanks for waiting with me.

LOU: No problem, I ain't that tired.

JANIE: I gotta get used to this. I was fallin' asleep in the bathrooms.

LOU: Ya know the guys; we take shifts sleeping. Two-hour shifts. I got last shift, so it's hard for me to get to sleep after I get off.

JANIE: I got a second wind. I was really tired and all a sudden I just kept goin'. Now I don't even know if I'll get to sleep either.

LOU: It's a good job, though. Even if it makes ya' sleep crazy.

JANIE: I'm lucky ta get it. I been outta work for four months. It's like shit out there, lookin' for work.

LOU: Who did ya know?

JANIE: Whatta ya mean?

LOU: How'd ya get the job?

JANIE: An old friend of mine got a job down at the office—secretary like.

LOU: You shouldn't worry. The supervisor comes maybe once a month. We hear about it 'cause he hits the downtown building first, then they call us up.

JANIE: No surprise stuff? Last place I worked they had surprise checks all the time.

LOU: That must be a bitch.

JANIE: One day I ain't in, the bastard he comes.

LOU: That's no problem here. Sure they come a lot in the day, but they don't like to come at night.

JANIE: I was worried about the hours— city at night and stuff.

LOU: Ya get used to them.

JANIE: Nah, I mean taking the train this early in the morning. I hear the stories.

LOU: How far you gotta go?

JANIE: Downtown.

LOU: Just stay right next to the conductor and you'll be down.

JANIE: It's almost light. It ain't too bad.

LOU: Nah, it ain't too bad… Sometimes I watch the sun go up on my way home—really nice… Hey, do you like movies?

JANIE: Love 'em.

LOU: You wanna see one? When you got time.

JANIE: Like when?

LOU: I don't know, whenever.

JANIE: I guess.

LOU: If you don't wanna, I ain't pushin'.

JANIE: Nah, I like to go.

LOU: What kinda movies you like?

JANIE: Funny ones.

LOU: Train ain't gonna come any faster by staring in a black hole.

JANIE: I like the breeze. My house is murder.

LOU: Sit down, take a load off your feet. *(He gets up and stands next to her.)* I'll watch and you sit.

JANIE: Thanks a lot for waitin' with me... Maybe when I get ta know the girls better, they give me a ride... That girl Maria's got a car, don't she?

LOU: That bitch?

JANIE: She seemed nice.

LOU: She drive you alright—charge ya a buck and half for it too... Besides, really, I don't mind waiting.

JANIE: I seen her and Julio.

LOU: Yeah, they got a thing... Both married, though maybe it's 'cause they're so bored... Hey looka' that.

JANIE: Where?

LOU: There.

JANIE: It's the size a my cat...Jesus, that's disgusting.

LOU: Rats don't sleep. They prowl around all night lookin' for scraps a shit... Once Julio was peeing in the cellar. Ya see we got like this drain ditch that's got water flowin' in it. And Julio is peeing, when all of a sudden this rat comes jumpin' up snappin' at his pecker. He comes back screamin' his Puerto Rican balls off... We cracked up. I think that's got ta be the funniest shit yet... When we got floods, I tell ya, I'm scared to take a step cause I might step on one of 'em. I don't know how those sewer workers do it. Make good money, though. City job—that's the job ta get.

JANIE: We gotta clean floods?

LOU: Nah, they send the guys down there with hoses and pumps, clean out all the shit. Just when it gets hot like this. The rats, they go for swims ta cool down. There ain't no A C. down there. It's murder, it smells like shit, pure shit.

JANIE: I hate rats and roaches... Bastards just won't die.

LOU: Survivors them rats...mostly in the city, but...

JANIE: I got a cat...with little tiger stripes. Her name's Atlas. She runs 'em all down for me. Just when she kills 'em she gives 'em to me. Like presents that is.

LOU: Sounds like a good cat.

JANIE: She's sick.

LOU: What's a matta with `im?

JANIE: I had her for months now. All she does is sit in the corner and scratch. Then when I go grab her she screams like a baby. It's so loud it makes me cry.

LOU: Ya take`er to a vet?

JANIE: I can't touch`er. And she won't eat nothin'. I just...it worries me sick. I don't know what's wrong with'er.

LOU: Ya' should call the A S P C A, they'll knock'er out or somethin' ta take`er.

JANIE: I'm just... I don't wan' `er to be dyin' or nothin'. If it wasn't for the cat I be crazy now.

LOU: My old man's sick. It worries me about him dyin' all the time. I take care of `im though. Real good care. He lives downstairs in the house 'cause he can't walk so good. The stairs and all.

JANIE: Ya' live with anybody else?

LOU: Nah, just me and the old man. That's it.

JANIE: Just me and my cat.

LOU: I don't mean to be nosy or nothin'. But somebody said you're married or somethin' like that.

JANIE: I'm married...I don't know what he's at...or where...yeah, but I'm married. Church too.

LOU: I mean, I didn't see no ring.

JANIE: I took it off.

LOU: Ya' still go to a movie, won't ya?

JANIE: Sure... He was no good, that's all. Run around at night and was always slappin' me. No beatin' or nothin'. He wasn't a wife beater or nothin'. Just lil' slaps here and there. They stung, but they never hurt, more like bites or somethin'.

LOU: I ain't never been married... I had some girlfriends, sure. Some in high school. But nothin' now...I mean, I ain't special, I know that. It ain't no big deal.

JANIE: Don't say that.

LOU: Nah, it's okay. I ain't stupid. I know I ain't good lookin'. It don't bother me none.

JANIE: You look fine.

LOU: I bet you look fine all made up and stuff.

JANIE: I looked fine once... Ya' see this? *(She touches the scar on her face.)* Ya' see it? I fell and cut myself. It don't go away. They say, though, for two grand they take it off. But I seen pictures of it gone wrong. Ladies with big lumpy faces. Sometimes it ain't so good.

LOU: I didn't wanna ask ya'.

JANIE: It's alright.

LOU: You hardly notice it.

JANIE: Thanks.

LOU: Everybody's got scars. I got one right here on my side.

JANIE: From what?

LOU: Well, nothin'... It was a fight. A guy got this knife.

JANIE: —Me too.

LOU: You too, what?

JANIE: I wish this train would be here already.

LOU: You got beat up or somethin'?

JANIE: I don't wanna talk about it.

LOU: Sorry. I didn't mean to...you know. I don't mean to be nosy.

JANIE: I was mugged. That's all.

LOU: Train?

JANIE: Yeah, my husband was supposed to pick me up. But he never showed. Probably out with some piece of shit.

LOU: Sorry.

JANIE: I'm sorry. You don't gotta hear this.

LOU: It's alright. I'm good at listenin'.

JANIE: Where'd you fight? How'd it happen?

LOU: I got stabbed.

JANIE: Where?

LOU: Well...I been in prison for a little while. Nothin' major, ya see. Like I didn't kill nobody or nothin'. I just sold a little dope, everybody was doin' it.

JANIE: Must be horrible.

LOU: No matta what you do in your life, never ever go to prison. People gettin' raped and stabbed all over the place.

JANIE: How long?

LOU: Seven months. Seven stinkin' months in torture. Place like that it tries ta kill ya. They keep hittin' you right in here, in your heart, till you're nothin' but muscle... They try to take your heart out.

JANIE: But you're alright?

LOU: I got scars you can't see. But I kept my heart...I did a lot of readin'. A lot. I mean I took advantage of it. You know my favorite writer has got to be Stephen King, and Sidney Sheldon is good too. But that's mostly woman stuff... Ya' know when there's a cool breeze I sit in the garden and read all afternoon. Sure, I watch the ballgame and I like to play the lottery. But after the hole, I tell ya', I just like to sit and read in the garden and watch the sky...Mr King has got to be one of the greatest livin' writers of our time. I mean I read so many of his I started over. And I seen scarier shit in prison, but I still like that scary stuff.

JANIE: I don't read much. Watch a lot of T V... They let you watch T V in prison?

LOU: Sure, they got T V rooms, but you gotta watch what the big shits say. Some kiss-asses got their own T Vs.

JANIE: You had a cellmate?

LOU: Yeah, and we gotta shit in the open too. And people are jerkin' off all over the place. Anything else you wanna know?

JANIE: Sorry.

LOU: It's okay... I guess ain't too many people been to prison. Shit, we had rats there, big things, could kill ya.

JANIE: Sounds awful.

LOU: Not only sounds awful, taste, smells and feels awful. It's the worst. But look, I got me a good job. Shit,

I don't mind bein' a janitor. Somebody's gotta clean the shit the bastards leave.

JANIE: They are pigs.

LOU: The more expensive the building, the bigger the corporation, the more they don't give a shit. Do whatever they like, don't care for nothin'.

JANIE: Any crazy stuff happen?

LOU: Craziest is when we found these polaroids of some vice-president dressed in drag. Angelo, he used to work here, he turned them in, and he got fired.

JANIE: Gotta learn to keep your mouth shut, Angelo.

LOU: No shit, we just get paid to pick the shit up that falls. And that's all I do. Pick up the shit, keep things clean and in order. That's hard enough.

JANIE: But rats.

LOU: Hey, your cat been in any fights with rats?

JANIE: Come to think of it, she did get cut up and came in one day. She'd been fightin'. Thought it was a dog, she's always fightin' them.

LOU: Maybe she got some rat poison in'er or somethin' like that.

JANIE: I didn't think of it.

LOU: Seen a rat with poison in'im, wouldn't die. He just screamin' and kickin' all over.

JANIE: Friend of mine says that's when cats screw. When the man cat comes out her he's got these scales that open and rip her down there, so no other cat can be screwin' her after him. Now, she says maybe somethin' like that happened to the cat and she got screwed up bad.

LOU: Shit. Wait. Ya mean the man cat he comes, rips her up like that and leaves her.

JANIE: That's why ya' hear'em screamin' late at night like that.

LOU: Imagine people were like that.

JANIE: Some are.

LOU: I get it... You know what your cat needs? A garden. I live right across the river and the cats out there, they do a lot better than city cats. Once a whole bunch of'em were born in my garden, little wild though, but I fed'em anyways.

JANIE: Must be nice out there.

LOU: It's a nice house.

JANIE: You got sisters and brothers?

LOU: Just me and the old man... We got a piano. I play a little. Not too good, but I play some.

JANIE: That's nice, like a real family, like.

LOU: You should come out and see it.

JANIE: How'd ya' family take goin' ta' prison?

LOU: I thought you were gonna forget about that.

JANIE: I'm sorry.

LOU: ...You wanna know somethin'? What killed my father? The day they came to my house and arrested me. I seen my father die. My mother, she was gone since I was little. My dad, he raised me, did a good job. Then he sees me get busted and he just falls and dies. His face gone right in front of me... In prison I crawled around like an animal. They wanted to make me an animal, but I wouldn't let'em... I go home after work and I make him a nice breakfast, and we sit in front of the T V and he's good. His foot, it's all messed up, but I take good care of'im. And before I go to work I make him some dinner, some bread, a little wine and he's happy. I mean he don't say nothin' much no more. So it's the little things that make'im good. I treat'em real good. I mean, he worked so hard. He deserves it, don't he?

JANIE: You must be a good son.

LOU: It's hard on a man when he gets a stroke. He don't feel like a man no more.

JANIE: But he's got you.

LOU: But who do I got? It's like I'm always puttin' things in order. Since prison I'm pickin' up pieces. But it don't work. It's always more shit fallin'.

JANIE: *(Pause)* I bought a six hundred-piece jigsaw puzzle, and you can't believe it, seven pieces were missing. Pissed me off. But I put the five hundred ninety-three together and it didn't look half bad.

LOU: What if your husband comes back?

JANIE: I hope the rat dies.

LOU: Some rats are just plain ole' Guinea pigs, you know that.

JANIE: Not this rat... He ain't comin' back, he's probably in some whore's lap right now. The misery he put me through. If someone could just repay him.

LOU: Did he cut you up?

JANIE: Why do you say that?

LOU: I just thought of it.

JANIE: I was mugged.

LOU: By him?

JANIE: It don't make no difference. If I'd rather it be I was mugged. I'd rather it be I was mugged!

LOU: I didn't do nothin' really. Somebody gave me the dope. I walked three blocks and gave it to somebody else. I didn't do nothin'.

JANIE: And you went to jail.

LOU: It was so fast.

JANIE: You're a nice guy.

LOU: You're nice too.

JANIE: I'm glad we're workin' together.

LOU: It's a good job. Once you learnin' how to do it, you get a lot of free time.

JANIE: For what?

LOU: You get five bucks a rat… But I don't think you'll be doin' that.

JANIE: I'm tired of catchin' rats.

LOU: Hey, you wanna have breakfast?

JANIE: Where?

LOU: *(Pause)* Come home with me.

JANIE: I got my cat…I'm tired.

LOU: Look, this train ain't never gonna come. Come on, you can see my garden.

JANIE: I really can't.

LOU: I'll borrow my neighbor's car and we will go get her.

JANIE: I don't know.

LOU: I like you. I like you a lot.

JANIE: Yeah, but…

LOU: I ain't a bad guy. I'm tellin' you, I'm soft and furry to curl up to.

(JANIE *takes a look. Pause. She looks for the train. She looks at* LOU.)

JANIE: I don't think this train is ever gonna come.

LOU: My train's upstairs. It goes across the river... It's cooler over there, there's a breeze, you can see the sky.
(JANIE *looks at* LOU. *She looks for the train. She looks at him. She pauses. She moves towards him and grabs his hand.*)
(*The lights fade as they leave together.*)
LOUNGE SINGER: (*To a* WAITER) Not that kind a match. I'm already smokin'. (*To the audience*) You think that's a stretch?
You shoulda seen her dress.
But, I don't wanna talk about my sex life, to—
Oh, enough of this. You want to know what Trudy's real name is? Rebecca. And we got back together too many times to remember. And I don't even know why she left the last time. A slip of the tongue. A thing not said. That's the truth. While I was workin' on my act, I forgot to work on my life. That's the truth. Rebecca and I split up for the same reason we all do, all
the wrong reasons.
(*He has a drink.*)
TO HAVE THE COURAGE TO JUMP. TO BE THE WIND, WEIGHTLESS. TO FLY THROUGH THE SKY. TO REST WHERE YOU WANT AND START WHERE YOU WANT.
To find her and toss her hair a bit.
If it was just so simple.
As simple as the wind.
If you wanna find me, I'll be on streets tonight like every night. Watching people, loving and living, waiting for the sun to rise, so I can go to sleep....
This is a song for those brave enough to hug, and hold, in those nights when the heat won't allow it.
(*He sings a song. He holds up his drink.*)
A drink to mediocrity.

To compromises that haunt you like a desperate kiss.
To casual sex.
To lowered expectations.
To the word "okay."
To the fast buck.
To Hollywood, television, and commercials.
To sound bites.
To the savings and loan.
To coffee table books.
To instant coffee, decaf cappucino and non-dairy creamers.
To microwaves.
To fast food.
To shopping malls.
To easy listening.
To museum posters.
To self-indulgence, self-involvement, and self-promotion.
To fear.
To reputation over courage.
To plot over drama.
To costumes over character.
To set over atmosphere.
To coulda been over what was.
To acting over feelings.
To love songs over love.
To Trudy over Becky...
To lying to yourself.
To my act.
To you all, I say.
If you bathe in mediocrity, you stink of mediocrity.
(He drinks.)
Thanks for coming. I'll see you tomorrow night.
(Lights dim.)

LOUNGE SINGER: ...Get out, have a long drink and slow cigarette. And go home, put the air conditioner on high, and warm yourselves up.

END OF PLAY